# Oracle Ultimate DBA
# Interview Questions

By: ORACOOKBOOK.com

Oracle Ultimate DBA Interview Questions
ISBN: 1-933804-26-2

Please visit our website at www.oracookbook.com

# TABLE OF CONTENTS

# Question 01:  Error while adding database

When trying to add database to tree and to network, the following error read while trying to connect them:

Failed to parse tnsnames.ora file
Error: 100--NLNV-NLNV String format Error

**A.** A syntax error occurred somewhere in your TNSNAMES.ORA file. Delete all entries in your TNSNAMES.ORA and start adding them back one-by-one until you find the entry that is responsible for the error.

# Question 02:  Can't login to EM

I did a basic install of Oracle 10g (standard) and installed a starter database. After install, via the EM console, the database did not start.
After clicking the start button, it asked for both the OS and Database user and password. For OS, I use 'Administrator' and password and for Database, I tried SYS and password but it still won't register.

How can I successfully login to EM?

**A.** The following procedures are suggested:

1. Install a Firefox 1.5 to upgrade your browser.

2. After completing installation and enter EM for the first time, you have to scroll to the bottom of the screen and "agree" to the eula a to continue using EM again. Re-install using UI.

3. Start lsnrctl start and emctl start dbconsole;
http:// localhost:1158/em for 10g

# Question 03: Unable to start enterprise manager for Oracle

I have two oracle 10g database:
[1]orcl < --- (first instance created)
[2]sunilhcl < --- (second instance)

For the first database, I wrote this link:
http://10.103.93.86:5501/em

The address bar of web page enterprise manager is in progress and also shows the name of database to which it is connected. What link should be written in the address bar of the web page if I want to start enterprise manager for oracle?

**A.** Reset the configuration file listener.ora by dbca.

Below is my listener.ora:

# listener.ora Network Configuration File:
/opt/oracle/product/10.2.0/network/admin/listener.ora
# Generated by Oracle configuration tools.

SID_LIST_LISTENER =
(SID_LIST =
(SID_DESC =
(SID_NAME = PLSExtProc)
(ORACLE_HOME = /opt/oracle/product/10.2.0)
(PROGRAM = extproc)
)
(SID_DESC =
(GLOBAL_DBNAME = orcl)
(ORACLE_HOME = /opt/oracle/product/10.2.0)
(SID_NAME = orcl)
)
)

LISTENER =
(DESCRIPTION_LIST =
(DESCRIPTION =

```
(ADDRESS = (PROTOCOL = IPC)(KEY = EXTPROC))
(ADDRESS = (PROTOCOL = TCP)(HOST = db31)(PORT =
1521))
)
)
```

## Question 04:  Failed to start Oracle 10g EM console

When I start up my Oracle 10gR2 console, it gives an error message alert saying:

"Windows could not start the OracleDbConsoleorcl on local computer. For more info, review the System Event Log"

I check the event log and it says:

"System log
The OracleDBConsoleorcl service terminated with service-specific error 2 (0x2)"

"Application log
Agent process exited abnormally during initialization"

Everything is running fine but I can't have my Oracle console up.

What procedure is needed to install my Oracle again?


**A.** You should change the IP back to what it was when you installed Oracle. If the Network cable is disconnected then unplug that cable, start DBConsole and then attach the cable again.

# Question 05:   EM Agent problem

I've got a problem with an agent installed on a w2000 server.
The host and the listener are running and databases are
discovered normally and following agent, everything is up. In
the grid control, database seems down and I don't understand
why.

2005-11-10 11:07:01 Thread-3216 Starting Agent 10.1.0.3.0 from
G:\oracle\product\10.1.0\em_1 (00701)
2005-11-10 11:07:01 Thread-3216 [Adapter Framework]
InstanceProperty (OidRepSchemaName) is marked OPTIONAL
but is being used (00506)
2005-11-10 11:07:02 Thread-3216 ParseError:
File=G:\oracle\product\10.1.0 \em_1\sysman\admin\metadata\
oracle_bc4j.xml, Line=486, Msg=attribute NAME in
<CategoryProp> cannot be NULL (01006)
2005-11-10 11:07:03 Thread-3216 Undefined column name
EFFICIENCY__BYTES_SAVED_WITH_COMPRESSION__AV
G_PER_SEC_SINCE_START in expression
EFFICIENCY__BYTES_SAVED_WITH_COMPRESSION__AV
G_PER_SEC_SINCE_START/1024/1024 (00104)
2005-11-10 11:07:12 Thread-3216 EMAgent started successfully
(00702)
2005-11-10 11:14:01 Thread-3216 EMAgent normal shutdown
(00703)

Environment: Grid under Windows2003 - 10.1.0.3
Target Machine: W2000 with oracle 8.1.7.3

How do I find my emagent.log?

**A.** The error is not platform specific to Windows. I am seeing
the same problem on Redhat Linux 4 U2 x86_64 using 10.2.0.1
agent (no databases running on the server yet) with the grid
running on 10.2.0.1.0 on Redhat Linux 4 U2 i386. Just expand
on this thread.

## Question 06: OEM in Oracle10G does not start

I type and enter this in my browser:
http://localhost:1158/em

At first, I only get this line:
java.lang.numberFormatException: For input string: "7.0B"

When I go to:
http://localhost:1158/em/console/logon/logon and log on the next page, I get the following errors:

500 Internal Server Error
java.lang.NumberFormatException: For input string: "7.0B"
at
java.lang.NumberFormatException.forInputString(NumberFor matException.java:48)
at
java.lang.FloatingDecimal.readJavaFormatString(FloatingDecim al.java:1207)
at java.lang.Float.valueOf(Float.java:205)
at java.lang.Float.<init>(Float.java:289)
at
oracle.sysman.emSDK.util.http.UserAgentUtil.getBrowserInfo(U serAgentUtil.java:300)
at
oracle.sysman.emSDK.util.http.UserAgentUtil.isUserAgentWind owsCE(UserAgentUtil.java:198)
at
oracle.sysman.emSDK.svlt.EMServletUtil.isEm2goApp(EMServl etUtil.java:178)
at oracle.sysman.eml.app.Console.doGet(Console.java:184)
at javax.servlet.http.HttpServlet.service(HttpServlet.java:740)
at javax.servlet.http.HttpServlet.service(HttpServlet.java:853)
at com.evermind[Oracle Application Server Containers for J2EE 10g
(9.0.4.1.0)].server.http.ResourceFilterChain.doFilter(ResourceFi lterChain.java:65)

at
oracle.sysman.emSDK.svlt.EMRedirectFilter.doFilter(EMRedire
ctFilter.java:101)
at com.evermind[Oracle Application Server Containers for J2EE
10g
(9.0.4.1.0)].server.http.EvermindFilterChain.doFilter(Evermind
FilterChain.java:16)
at
oracle.sysman.db.adm.inst.HandleRepDownFilter.doFilter(Han
dleRepDownFilter.java:138)
at com.evermind[Oracle Application Server Containers for J2EE
10g
(9.0.4.1.0)].server.http.EvermindFilterChain.doFilter(Evermind
FilterChain.java:20)
at
oracle.sysman.eml.app.ContextInitFilter.doFilter(ContextInitFilt
er.java:269)
at com.evermind[Oracle Application Server Containers for J2EE
10g
(9.0.4.1.0)].server.http.ServletRequestDispatcher.invoke(Servlet
RequestDispatcher.java:600)
at com.evermind[Oracle Application Server Containers for J2EE
10g
(9.0.4.1.0)].server.http.ServletRequestDispatcher.forwardIntern
al(ServletRequestDispatcher.java:317)
at com.evermind[Oracle Application Server Containers for J2EE
10g
(9.0.4.1.0)].server.http.HttpRequestHandler.processRequest(Htt
pRequestHandler.java:793)
at com.evermind[Oracle Application Server Containers for J2EE
10g
(9.0.4.1.0)].server.http.HttpRequestHandler.run(HttpRequestH
andler.java:270)
at com.evermind[Oracle Application Server Containers for J2EE
10g
(9.0.4.1.0)].server.http.HttpRequestHandler.run(HttpRequestH
andler.java:112)
at com.evermind[Oracle Application Server Containers for J2EE
10g
(9.0.4.1.0)].util.ReleasableResourcePooledExecutor$MyWorker.
run(ReleasableResourcePooledExecutor.java:192)
at java.lang.Thread.run(Thread.java:534)

I am using winxp home edition. All my services are running even my sqlplus. My application servers' first page is displayed but when I click on one of the examples, I get an http 404 error.

How do I correctly start OEM in Oracle10G?

**A.** Use the O/S credentials and provide the 'Log on as a batch job' privilege: The following procedure should work:

1. Go to control panel/administrative tools.
   a. click on "local security policy"
   b. click on "local policies"
   c. click on "user rights assignments"
   d. double click on "log on as a batch job"
   e. click on "add" and add the user that was entered in the "normal   username" or "privileged username" section of the EM Console.

2. Go to the Preferences link in the EM GUI.
   a. click on Preferred Credentials (link on the left menu)
   b. under "Target Type: Host" click on "set credentials"
   c. enter the OS user who has logon as a batch job privilege into the
      "normal username" and "normal password" fields

3. Test the connection.
   a. while in the Set Credentials window, click on "Test"

## Question 07: Oracle 10g database and Oracle 10 client in same pc

How do I install oracle 10g database and oracle 10 client in the same pc?

**A.** You can install both in the same pc but you don't need to have a separate client installation in the same machine (unless you are using different tools like forms/reports).

Install server and any/all components you want.
Make sure you install oracle sqlplus, etc. to create database.

However, you cannot put it in the same dir and set a classpath or oracle home. Every client has to be in a different
ORACLE_HOME.
Read documentation.
http://download-
east.oracle.com/docs/cd/B19306_01/install.102/b14318/toc.ht
m

Any oracle product that needs ORACLE_HOME cannot be installed in same directory. You need to use different directories.

## Question 08:   Unable to log in to console

We stopped getting emails for job starts/completes and could no longer log into the OEM console. It hangs after hitting Submit. The scheduled jobs have stop running as well. We try to stop and start the Oracle Management server with oemctl start oms but it just hangs there. We are running 9.2.0 on UNIX.

How can we log into our OEM console again?

**A.** Check on your access permissions on the UNIX. Try to start the OMS service with another UNIX user.

# Question 09:  Unable to start OMS

I recently installed oracle9.2.0.1.0 on redhat el as4 and successfully installed oracle and created a db. The oem console works well but when I try to start oms (I have created the repository), it failed. The system gave out the following information:

Please check the file /opt/ora9/product/9.2/sysman/log/oms.nohup for more details. Terminated

Starting the Oracle Management Server:

Error starting Oracle Management Server. ORBSingleton: access deniedjava.lang.SecurityException: ORBSingleton: access denied
at
com.sun.corba.se.internal.corba.ORBSingleton.connect(ORBSingleton.java:330)
at
oracle.sysman.vxn.VxnNamingContext.<init>(VxnNamingContext.java:285)
at
oracle.sysman.vxn.VxnNamingContext.getNewContext(VxnNamingContext.java:222)
at
oracle.sysman.vxn.VxnNamingService.getInitialContext(VxnNamingService.java:1072)
at
oracle.sysman.vxn.VxnNamingService.enableBootstrap(VxnNamingService.java:1080)
at
oracle.sysman.vxn.VxnNamingService.init(VxnNamingService.java:238)
at
oracle.sysman.vxn.VxnNamingService.getNamingService(VxnNamingService.java:103)
at
oracle.sysman.vxn.VxnNamingService.getNamingService(VxnNamingService.java:112)

at
oracle.sysman.vxa.VxaAppServer.initServer(VxaAppServer.java:
3417)
at
oracle.sysman.vxa.VxaAppServer.main(VxaAppServer.java:3048
)
OMS exited on Mon Oct 24 09:25:49 CST 2005 with return value
56
Could not start management server. Initialization failure
\nManagement server startup failed. Check the file
/opt/ora9/product/9.2/sysman/log/oms.nohup for details

How do I properly start OMS?

**A.** In oemctl file, make sure your PATH.check have correct
values in ORACLE_HOME.

# Question 10:  Unable to login to the database

I have successfully installed Oracle 10g at a client site. When I tried to launch the enterprise manager to create a schema: xxxx:5500\em, the page did not load. Then I tried "xxxx:5500\em\console\logon\logon and got the initial logon screen to the database ORCL.  I entered the username & password and click on the login button, nothing happened.  I tried sys, sysman, system, but was also of no use.

How can I login to the database?

**A.**  Do either or both of the following process:

a. Check if DB Control is running (if you can, restart it). Also, clear your
   browser's cache as you may be getting an old copy of the page.

b. >sqlplus

SQL*Plus: Release 10.1.0.2.0 - Production on Wed Oct 26 11:41:19 2005
Copyright (c) 1982, 2004, Oracle. All rights reserved.

Enter user-name: sys / as sysdba
Enter password: <anything works>

Connected to:
Oracle Database 10g Enterprise Edition Release 10.1.0.2.0 - 64bit Production
With the Partitioning, OLAP and Data Mining options

SQL>
Now alter user <user> identified by <your new password>;

# Question 11: Oracle 10.2G: e-mail events every minute

Is it possible to receive events every minute via EM with an Oracle 10.2G?

**A.** Events are mailed out every time ADDM runs (after each AWR snapshot). Try to set this:

SQL> SELECT * FROM dba_hist_wr_control;

```
    DBID SNAP_INTERVAL      RETENTION          TOPNSQL
---------- -------------------- -------------------- ----------
966815583 +00000 01:00:00.0   +00007 00:00:00.0
DEFAULT
```

SQL>
SQL> BEGIN
  2
DBMS_WORKLOAD_REPOSITORY.MODIFY_SNAPSHOT_SE
TTINGS(
  3      retention => 43200,
  4      interval  => 10
  5  );
  6 END;
  7 /

PL/SQL procedure successfully completed.

SQL>
SQL> SELECT * FROM dba_hist_wr_control;

```
    DBID SNAP_INTERVAL      RETENTION          TOPNSQL
---------- -------------------- -------------------- ----------
966815583 +00000 00:10:00.0   +00030 00:00:00.0
DEFAULT
```

SQL>

The intervals cannot go below 10 minutes.

# Question 12: Shutting down database using Enterprise Manager

After shutting down an oracle9i database using Oracle9i Enterprise Manager, I noticed that the Service window still shows "Started" for the status of "OracleServiceDB_name" service. What does start and stop OracleServiceDB_name in Services window do?

**A.** Shutting down an Oracle database does not mean stopping Oracle service also. It will just close the database and free space from physical memory. Oracle service starts automatically when one starts the machine.

# Question 13: Unable to connect to management server

I have installed orcle9i standard edition on Windows XP and was successful in logging on to the Oracle Enterprise manager using sysman/oem_temp Management server=localhost. I even changed the password of sysman to manager.

I tried to login again using sysman/manager Mgmt server=localhost but got this error "VTK1000 - Unable to connect to mgmt server".

I checked the "My computer-services" option and there it shows Mgmt server status=blank and startup type = Manual.

What is the correct procedure that will connect me to the management server?

**A.** OEM shoots VTK-1000 error if OMS service has not started or OEM repository doesn't exist. As per you posting, it seems that you didn't start the service. Do so in control panel/services and start the services for OEM, Intelligent agent, etc., and set it to automatic.

# Question 14:  Wrong password for user

I have installed Oracle 10g on Windows XP. I have an administrator account without a password, but my username on windows xp system is Peter. I tried to follow the steps for starting up the database:

Go to Control Panel-->Administrative Tools-->Local Security Policy-->Local Policies-->User Rights Assignment-->you will see in the policy as "Log on as a batch Job-->right click-->Properties-->add user or groups-->give your OS username.

I set Peter as my OS username but the database won't start after going back to the Enterprise Manager.

How do I initiate the database?

**A.** You have to provide the 'Log on as a batch job' privilege:

1. Go to control panel/administrative tools
    a. click on "local security policy"
    b. click on "local policies"
    c. click on "user rights assignments"
    d. double click on "log on as a batch job"
    e. click on "add" and add the user that was entered in the "normal
    username" or "p rivileged username" section of the EM Console.

2. Go to the Preferences link in the EM GUI
    a. click on Preferred Credentials (link on the left menu)
    b. under "Target Type: Host" click on "set credentials"
    c. enter the OS user who has logon as a batch job privilege into the
    "normal username" and "normal password" fields

3. Test the connection
    a. while in the Set Credentials window, click on "Test"

# Question 15: Oracle Intelligent Agent

How does one start Intelligent Agent for data gathering if using a Solaris 9, Oracle 10.1.2? Do you need a database to store the gathered information?

**A.** Run the Intelligent Agent in the XP Pro box at my office instead of going into the computer room whenever you want to manage Oracle.

Use eXcursion which is an Xterminal program and set ssh as a program to tunnel X11. Then via ssh set the display xxx.xxx.xxx.xxx (export DISPLAY=<ip address>). Then in a ssh window key in 'netscape.'

Another procedure to start will be:

emctl start dbconsole
or when using Grid Control:
emctl start agent;

# Question 16: OMS problem

I have an OEM set up and was running correctly for a few weeks. When I needed to restart the OEM and exited, it froze the computer.

When I tried to start the management server process, it failed. The following error messages are found in the Application Event Log:

-The service is entering into production run mode.
-The process termination failed for JRE. %2
-The service has terminated abnormally. See the file *\*\*\oms.nohup for details.

The oms.nohup file showed the ff:

Error starting Oracle Management Server. VXA -2020 : Error encountered when service [vdp] attempted to export its servicesOEMCTRL for Windows NT: Version 2.2.0.0.0 Copyright (c) 1998, 2000, Oracle Corporation. All rights reserved.
Starting the Oracle Management Server... [main][2005-7-6:12:9:39:46] VdbSession.processError: errorCode >1033<
[main][2005-7-6:12:9:39:46] VdbSession.processError: errorMsg >ORA-01033: ORACLE initialization or shutdown in progress
<
[main][2005-7-6:12:9:39:46] VdbSession.processError: database connection error
[main][2005-7-6:12:9:49:250] VdbSession.processError: errorCode >1033<
[main][2005-7-6:12:9:49:250] VdbSession.processError: errorMsg >ORA-01033: ORACLE initialization or shutdown in progress
<
[main][2005-7-6:12:9:49:250] VdbSession.processError: database connection error
VXA -3008 : Starting OMS Services, Wait.

[main][2005-7-6:12:10:45:93] VDP PANIC: SQL exception caught inside VdpPingServiceImpl.redistributeNodesOnStartUp() exception VdbSQLException{wstring reason="ORA-06553: PLS-213: package STANDARD not accessible\n";long oracleError=6553;long errorCode=3;wstring sqlStmt="";}
at
oracle.sysman.vdb.VdbStatement.processError(VdbStatement.java:368)
at
oracle.sysman.vdb.VdbCallableStatement.execute(VdbCallableStatement.java:223)
at
oracle.sysman.v db.VdbAutoCommitSession.executeQuery(VdbAutoCommitSession.java:336)
at
oracle.sysman.vdp.VdpPingServiceImpl.redistributeNodesOnStartUp(VdpPingServiceImpl.java:541)
at
oracle.sysman.vdp.VdpPingServiceImpl.exportServices(VdpPingServiceImpl.java:324)
at
oracle.sysman.vxa.VxaAppServer.startServices(VxaAppServer.java:1513)
at
oracle.sysman.vxa.VxaAppServer.main(VxaAppServer.java:2547)
[main][2005-7-6:12:10:45:734] VD-5251 : A system error has occurred inside [Pinging Service]: ORA-06553: PLS-213: package STANDARD not accessible

[main][2005-7-6:12:10:45:734] VXA -2021 :
OMS Service startup failed!
oracle.sysman.vxn.VxnBootstrapException: VXA -2020 : Error encountered when service [vdp] attempted to export its services
at
oracle.sysman.vxa.VxaAppServer.startServices(VxaAppServer.java:1514)
at
oracle.sysman.vxa.VxaAppServer.main(VxaAppServer.java:2547)

Error starting Oracle Management Server. VXA -2020 : Error encountered when service [vdp] attempted to export its services.

What steps should be done to start the OMS again?

**A.** It seems OMS is not happy with the database components, maybe the repository database is not available. Do a clean shutdown of all the services/database. Reboot the machine. Mount and open only the database that has the repository / oms components.

See whether you can establish a simple sql connection into this: Post the errors.
>> ORA-06553: PLS-213: package STANDARD not accessible
Try to compile the package SYS.STANDARD.
If this does not work;
Then, run $ORACLE_HOME/rdbms/admin/catalog.sql and catproc.sql logged in as SYS.
Try again.
Make sure you have done the ff:
1. All databases in all participating nodes are available.
2. Their listeners are available.
3. Their intelligent agents are available.
4. You can individually to a simple sql session.
5. Start OMS.

## Question 17: Connect to 10g OEM with Windows o/s authentication

How do you connect to Enterprise Manager DB Control using Windows o/s authentication?

**A.** Run the following procedure:
Start -> Programs -> Administrative
Tools -> Local Security Settings and add the user y ou need to the 'Log on as a batch job' policy.

# Question 18: ORA-00406: COMPATIBLE parameter

I'm having difficulty when creating a table with list partition ORA-00406:

COMPATIBLE parameter needs to be 9.2.0.0.0 or greater version of oracle. What I'm using is greater than 9.2.0.0.0 SQL*Plus: Release 9.2.0.1.0 - Production on Tue Sep 6 16:53:15 2005

Copyright (c) 1982, 2002, Oracle Corporation. All rights reserved.
Connected to:
Oracle9i Enterprise Edition Release 9.2.0.5.0 - 64bit Production With the Partitioning, OLAP and Oracle Data Mining options JServer Release 9.2.0.5.0 - Production

DDL command as follows:

CREATE TABLE CS_CASE_INFO_PART
(
CS_CASE_INFO_ID NUMBER(10) NOT NULL,
FINANCIER_ID VARCHAR2(75 BYTE) NOT NULL,
APPL_ID VARCHAR2(75 BYTE) NOT NULL,
CUST_ID VARCHAR2(75 BYTE) NOT NULL,
PRODUCT_ID VARCHAR2(45 BYTE) NOT NULL,
CUST_NAME VARCHAR2(195 BYTE) NOT NULL,
DPD NUMBER(3) NOT NULL,
INSTALLMENT_DUE_DATE DATE,
NO_OF_INST_OVERDUE NUMBER(,
AMOUNT_OVERDUE NUMBER(16,2),
MIN_AMOUNT_DUE NUMBER(16,2),
NO_OF_INST_OUTSTANDING NUMBER(,
AMOUNT_OUTSTANDING NUMBER(16,2),
GRACE_DAYS NUMBER(3),
GRACE_AMOUNT NUMBER(16,2),
HHNO VARCHAR2(60 BYTE),
TOTAL_CHARGES_OVERDUE NUMBER(16,2),
PRINCIPLE_OVERDUE NUMBER(16,2),

```
PRINCIPLE_OUTSTANDING NUMBER(16,2),
INTEREST_OVERDUE NUMBER(16,2),
INTEREST_OUTSTANDING NUMBER(16,2),
COLLECTION_CYCLE NUMBER(2),
BUCKET NUMBER(3),
QUEUE VARCHAR2(24 BYTE),
ZONE VARCHAR2(24 BYTE)
AGENCY VARCHAR2(24 BYTE),
DISBURSAL_DATE DATE,
WLL_NO VARCHAR2(20 BYTE),
LAFNO VARCHAR2(20 BYTE),
DUPLICATE_BILL_REQUEST VARCHAR2(1 BYTE),
BUCKET0 NUMBER(16,2),
OTAF_DATE DATE,
PLAN VARCHAR2(100 BYTE),
LTD_PMNT NUMBER(16,2),
NO_BILLS_RAISED NUMBER(10),
AGENT_CODE VARCHAR2(24 BY TE)
)
TABLESPACE DATA
PARTITION BY LIST(ZONE)
(
PARTITION CIRCLE_CAP VALUES('CAP')NOLOGGING,
PARTITION CIRCLE_CBB VALUES('CBB')NOLOGGING,
PARTITION CIRCLE_CBB VALUES('CCC')NOLOGGING,
PARTITION CIRCLE_CBB VALUES('CDL')NOLOGGING,
PARTITION CIRCLE_CBB VALUES('CGJ')NOLOGGING,
PARTITION CIRCLE_CBB VALUES('CKL')NOLOGGING,
PARTITION CIRCLE_CBB VALUES('CKN')NOLOGGING,
PARTITION CIRCLE_CBB VALUES('CMH')NOLOGGING,
PARTITION CIRCLE_CBB VALUES('CMP')NOLOGGING,
PARTITION CIRCLE_CBB VALUES('CMU')NOLOGGING,
PARTITION CIRCLE_CBB VALUES('CPJ')NOLOGGING,
PARTITION CIRCLE_CBB VALUES('CRJ')NOLOGGING,
PARTITION CIRCLE_CBB VALUES('CTN')NOLOGGING,
PARTITION CIRCLE_CBB VALUES('CUP')NOLOGGING,
PARTITION CIRCLE_CBB VALUES('CWB')NOLOGGING,
PARTITION CIRCLE_NULL VALUES(NULL)NOLOGGING,
PARTITION CIRCLE_UNKNOWN
VALUES(DEFAULT)NOLOGGING
);
```

How do I correct this error and find a compatible parameter?

**A.** Check the value of compatible in your parameter file with:

SQL> show parameter compatible

NAME TYPE VALUE
------------------------------------ ----------- ----------------------------
compatible string 9.2.0.0.0

If it is less than 9.2.0.0.0, then change this parameter to compatible string 9.2.0.0.0 and proceed as follows:

In your pfile you will find an entry for compatible parameter, which will look like this (it's an excerpt from my pfile, your pfile should contain value something like 9.0.2 or similar):

```
###########################################
# Miscellaneous
###########################################
compatible=9.2.0.0.0
```

Now change the pfile parameter to 9.2.0.0.0 value and save it.

Then startup the database with this pfile:

SQL> startup pfile=d:\oracle\ora92\....\pfile\init.ora

and then create spfile from this pfile,

SQL> create spfile from pfile;

# Question 19: Creating OMS

I have installed oracle 9i on windows 2000 server but fail to install OMS. I tried using OEM but also yielded negative results. How can I successfully create OMS in the system?

**A.** First, you need to update your Windows going to microsoft.com. This should be done until no more critical alerts and your Windows is updated with the critical patches.

Second, if you for example have 500 mb of Ram, use 4096MB of your disk space as virtual memory. This should be done going to the system properties, advance and configuring your virtual memory.

Third, install the OEM. If installing 10g, you have to know that you will not be seeing or browsing any database as you did in 9i, unless you have installed in each server where your databases resides the Enterprise Manager Agent 10g even though your database is 9i in the database that you want to monitor. Also, you should know that this will only function with databases version 8.1.7.4 --> Note the patch level and 9i.
Databases version 8.1.7.0 will not work. When installing the Enterprise Manager Agent in the servers where other database resides, you have to perform the following:

1. Stop the agent on the target node:

   "emctl stop agent"

2. Delete any pending upload files from the agent home.

```
rm -r $ORACLE_HOME/sysman/emd/state/*
rm -r $ORACLE_HOME/sysman/emd/collection/*
rm -r $ORACLE_HOME/sysman/emd/upload/*
rm $ORACLE_HOME/sysman/emd/lastupld.xml
rm $ORACLE_HOME/sysman/emd/agntstmp.txt
rm $ORACLE_HOME/sysman/emd/blackouts.xml
rm $ORACLE_HOME/sysman/emd/protocol.ini
```

3. Issue an agent clearstate from the agent home:

"emctl clearstate"

4. Start the agent.

"emctl start agent"

5. Force an upload to the OMS:

"emctl upload"

Status agent show it did upload to the
REPOSITORY_URL=http://<the name of your 10g
OEM>:7777/em/upload w/o issue

This will be uploaded automatically to your OEM version 10g.

## Question 20: Oracle 9i OEMC unable to login

I have installed Oracle 9i to my machine and tried to login to the Oracle Enterprise Management Console (OEMC). The default setting for the Administrator is sysman\oem_temp and the password is oem_temp.

I tried the defaults but they did not work. Where can I find my OEMC Administrator ID and Password? How can I log in?

**A.** You will find an OEM guide when installing the software. It creates an Administrator (Super Admin) ID and password. Once you have the correct Administrator and password and log in, the systems will ask you to change your password. You will be able now to log on to the OEMC.

## Question 21: Add/Remove Program

We install all our programs using Oracle Universal Installer, like OEM 9.2.0.1.0, Form/ Report Developer 6i from autorun. Can we see what is installed or listed in the Control Panel add/remove programs including Oracle Universal Installer?

**A.** Oracle programs are not listed in "Add/ Remove Programs" nor will you see Oracle Universal Installer. To see what was installed, start the installer and click o n "Installed Products".

Another way is to write regedit in the cmd console. Under the hykey_local_machine, you will see all installed products and software.

# Question 22: Agent fails to start

The following procedure was performed to start up agent:

$agentctl start

But the system showed:

DBSNMP for IBM/AIX RISC System/6000: Version 9.2.0.3.0 - Production on 15-AUG-2005 16:13:36

Copyright (c) 2003 Oracle Corporation. All rights reserved.

Starting Oracle Intelligent Agent...
Agent startup failed. Check
/oracle/app/product/9.2.0/network/log/dbsnmp.nohup for detail
$

view/oracle/app/product/9.2.0/network/log/dbsnmp.nohup

------------------------ Mon 15 Aug 16:13:36 2005 --------------------
----
Failed while initializing SNMP
Error initializing subsystems
Agent exited at Mon 15 Aug 16:13:36 2005 with return value 55

What is the correct way to enable Agent?

**A.** Go to your $ORACLE_HOME/network/agent directory.

Copy all files in that directory somewhere else for backup.

Delete all the *.q files and the services.ora file.

Now from the command line run agentctl start.

# Question 23: Problem with enterprise manager

I have an oracle 9i Enterprise Manager version. In this edition, I saw an Oracle Enterprise Manager in the oracle list of programs. I accidentally removed that shortcut from the programs list.

How do I retrieve back the OEM?

**A.** All the Oracle executables are stored at %ORACLE_HOME%\bin.

The location of EM is %ORACLE_HOME%\bin\oemapp.bat

If you want to launch OEM console then go to command prompt and write:

C:\> oemapp.bat console

This command to run the path should set to ORACLE_HOME\bin.

## Question 24: Enterprise manager for oracle 9i

Is it possible to download enterprise manager for oracle 9i from the internet? What is isqlplus?

**A.** The 9i Enterprise manager comes with the Oracle S/W itself, no way to download this individually.

An isqlplus is a tool provided to use Oracle from the browser. You can use it for transactions but can't do any administration activity. Write:

http://localhost/isqlplus in the browser of the server hosting Oracle and it will be ready for use.

# Question 25: Fire Trigger

I have a trigger that inserts a new value into a field after a row is committed. When ID is populated by the trigger and assigned a value say 10, that value is also automatically assigned to ProgessID (i.e. ProgressID = 10).

Is there a way I could create an insert trigger that inserts that number generated by the trigger into another field on the same row (e.g.
tblX has fields ID, ProgessID, Service)?

**A.** The following code should work perfectly:

```
BEGIN
 SELECT SVDB.S_114_2_TBLPROGRESSNOTE.nextval
  INTO :NEW.ID
  FROM dual;
 :NEW.ProgressID:=:NEW.ID;
END;
```

# Question 26:   Insufficient Privileges

I tried to create a clone database from our production system on our test system. We are using Solaris for both systems. The very old database files on the test box were deleted and stopped all the process associated with it. Basically, I wanted a "clean" environment to start with.

The production database was stopped and a complete cold backup was taken. These files were then copied over to the test box. I placed every file in the exact same location on the test box as they were on the production box. The db has a password file which was also copied over.  Prior to shutdown on the prod db, I issued the alter db backup control file to trace. This file was also copied over to the test box and modified accordingly to create a new db under a new name.

I have created an entry in the tnsnames.ora and listener.ora files for this new database.

The following code was performed to access the database:

```
-->export ORACLE_SID=TLE5
DACEDIT1(/db/mo1/oracle/product/8.1.7)
-->echo $ORACLE_SID
TLE5
DACEDIT1(/db/mo1/oracle/product/8.1.7)
-->sqlplus
```

SQL*Plus: Release 8.1.7.0.0 - Production on Mon Apr 10 15:48:14 2006

(c) Copyright 2000 Oracle Corporation. All rights reserved.

Enter user-name: sys/xxxxxx@TLE5 as sysdba
ERROR:
ORA-01031: insufficient privileges

And when I wrote the command ps -ef|grep "ora"
I got the following:

oracle 11400 1 0 13:41:09 ? 0:00 oracleTLE5 (LOCAL=NO)
oracle 5966 1 0 10:34:27 ? 0:01 orac leTLE5T2 (LOCAL=NO)

I keep getting the insufficient privileges message when I try to sign on as sys, what is the correct procedure?

**A.** Delete old password file and create a new one with a new password using ORAPWD utility.

Check the value of SQLNET.AUTHENTICATION_SERVICES = (NONE) in
$oracle_home/network/admin/sqlnet.ora

# Question 27: TNS: protocol adapter error

I'm trying to connect to my database named "NEWDB'. I was able to successfully connect with **SQLPLUS** but failed when I used **SQLPLUSW**.
This process was performed on the same machine.

The following error appeared:

SQL> connect sys/welcome123 as sysdba
ERROR:
ORA-12560: TNS protocol adapter error

How can I fix this?

**A.** Have you created Net Service name in TNSNAMES.ORA file?
If not,
open $oracle_home/network\admin\tnsnames.ora file and add service

e.g.:
TEST =
(DESCRIPTION =
(ADDRESS_LIST =
(ADDRESS = (PROTOCOL = TCP)(HOST = dbser)(PORT = 1522))
)
(CONNECT_DATA =
(SID = test)
(SERVER = DEDICATED)
)
)

Use TNSPING test to check if it is working. Then try to connect.

## Question 28: 9i OEM or OMS to manage 10g database

Can we use Oracle9i OEM and OMS to manage the Oracle10g databases?

**A.** No you can't. You need to use grid control or database control to manage 10G databases, depending on your requirements. On the other hand, you can use 10g Grid Control to manage 9i databases.

## Question 29: Data Dictionary View(s)

I have a certain table or view. I want to find out the granted select rights or execute rights on a certain function or procedure given to users.

Which Database Dictionary View(s) contain the information on the user's access rights to certain database objects?

**A.** The following command will give you the information you want:

    dba_tab_privs

## Question 30:  Rollback segment

We have 6 rollback segments in our database. How do I find the sizes of each rollback segments?

**A.** Use the following command:

dba_rollback_segs

# Question 31: Recovery help

I have a database running in archive log mode.

Time T1:
cold backup of the database was taken; All datafile,controlfile and redo log files.

Time T2:
New tablespace added.

Time T3:
Latest Control file and Latest datafiles are lost. But I have only latest Redo log files intact.

Also, I have all the archive log files since the last cold backup. The cold backup taken at Time T1 is also intact.

I tried recovering with latest redo log and the cold backup but got the following error:

SQL> recover database using backup controlfile;
ORA-00279: change 565321 generated at 04/06/2006 19:22:34 needed for thread 1
ORA-00289: suggestion :
E:\ORACLE\ORADATA\ARCHIVES\ARC00008.001
ORA-00280: change 565321 for thread 1 is in sequence #8

Specify log: {=suggested | filename | AUTO | CANCEL}
auto
ORA-00283: recovery session canceled due to errors
ORA-00600: internal error code, arguments: [3020], [8388697], [1], [8],
[12856], [16], [], []
ORA-10567: Redo is inconsistent with data block (file# 2, block# 89)
ORA-10564: tablespace UNDOTBS1
ORA-01110: data file 2:
'E:\ORACLE\ORADATA\STST\UNDOTBS01.DBF'
ORA-10560: block type 'KTU SMU HEADER BLOCK'

ORA-01112: media recovery not started

I'm tying to recover on a normal database with Oracle Release 9.2.0.1.0 version.

Is it possible to recover the database including the tablespace recently added at Time T2?
**A.** Yes, go to:

http://download-west.oracle.com/doc...arios.htm#14480

This site will explain and tell you what to do if you have online redo but no backup of new tablespace and datafile(s). However, if you are unsure of what you need to do, I would recommend opening a serverity 1 service request with Oracle Support. Make sure the online logs are applied manually. Automatic recovery will search for archived logs with the same log sequence numbers as the online logs.

# Question 32: Archived log files missing in Online Backup

**I have an Oracle DB backup on Tape (Version 9.2.0.4.0) and have an online backup.**

Only the datafiles and the controlfile can be restored. I do not have the archived log files that were generated during the online backup period.

How do I recover my DB and make it available?

**A.** Try to do incomplete recovery (point in time based or SCN based)
but you will loose all the data after some time. You cannot recover if you don't have the archives that were generated during the backup.

# Question 33: ORA-19760: error starting change tracking

I am using 10g R2 (64 bit) on Solaris 10 Sparc server with 24gig memory. The database is in archivelog mode and I am implementing RMAN on it. To use the new block tracking feature of RMAN, I run the following command:

alter database enable block change tracking using file '/oradump01/orcl/rman/track/btf.dbf';

But I got this error:

ERROR at line 1:
ORA-19760: error starting change tracking

When I checked the alert log file I got the following message:

alter database enable block change tracking using file '/oradump01/orcl/rman/track/btf.dbf'
Thu Apr 6 13:26:27 2006
Block change tracking file is current.
Starting background process CTWR
CTWR started with pid=18, OS id=22233
Thu Apr 6 13:26:33 2006
Errors in file
/orahome/admin/orcl/bdump/orcl_ctwr_22233.trc:
ORA-04031: unable to allocate 15613832 bytes of shared memory ("shared pool","unknown object","sga heap(1,0)","CTWR dba buffer")
Block change tracking service stopping.
Thu Apr 6 13:26:33 2006
Stopping background process CTWR
ORA-19760 signalled during: alter database enable block change tracking using file '/oradump01/orcl/rman/track/btf.dbf'...
Deleted file /oradump01/orcl/rman/track/btf.dbf

The shared memory setting for the server is:
set shmsys:shminfo_shmmax=0xffffffff --Maximum available

set shmsys:shminfo_shmmin=1
set shmsys:shminfo_shmseg=50

How do I operate the new block tracking feature of RMAN?

**A.** You need to set the shared memory settings and increase the shared pool database parameter.

# Question 34: Delete in multi-master replication

I want to do a manual deletion of records at any of the master site in a multi-master replication set up. Can this create any issues in propagation?

**A.** No, it will not create any issues in propagation. If you delete a record in one of the master sites, the deletes will be carried out in the other sites as well. If the master sites are identical, there shouldn't be any conflicts. You can always set up conflict resolutions methods if required.

## Question 35: 9i server and 10g client

I tried to have 9i server and 10g client on the same box but got a tnsora error and could not start the database. Is this possible or will it have conflict with any parameters?

**A.** Yes you can, but only if you are on windows. Be cautious as your PATH system environment variable will be changed following any oracle install. You may need to manually re-order it, depending on your requirements.

## Question 36: View oracle database installed on HP-UX from windows

I want to create DSN for Oracle database. Which type of driver should be added on a Windows machine? Will Win SQL work to view this database from windows?

**A.** You need to install Oracle client on your Windows pc and then have the tnsname.ora file containing an entry of the database you need to connect to. Then you can use sqlplus gui or any other tool to access the databases. For o dbc connection, you need to use the oracle driver or the microsoft odbc for Oracle.

# Question 37: ORA - 07217 errors

I am trying to connect to oracle database instance using sql plus on HP-UX machine. After giving username & password, the following error displayed:

ORA - 07217 error - sltln env variable not found

What steps should I do to correct this error?

**A.** Set your ORACLE_ID or use @db_name.

# Question 38: Configure GC to send alert message

We are using Diagnostics Pack, one of the 4 'optional' management packs available for Grid Control to monitor Dataguard in our environment.

Can we configure the GC to send alert/warning messages outside of the tool (email, pager, etc.) without using the Diagnostics pack?

**A.** Read about Notification Methods in the Grid Control manual (http://download-west.oracle.com/doc...htm#sthref1047). Grid Control will send email out of the box, but for pager, etc. you'll need to create an OS script on the management server and create a new method to run the script. Then associate the new method with a notification rule.

# Question 39:   Verify commit time

I am working with an oracle9i and have a large DB with more or less than 1.5 Tb. Now I can't use the database statpack or other package. Which v$ tables do I use to verify the commit time?

**A.** CAVEAT EMPTOR - the following is not very "scientific" since it mixes up wait stats from active sessions that have been running for very different lengths of time, but it does give a <u>feel</u> of what is not going on. You might want to comment out the "event NOT like" lines to begin with.

Use the following code:
```
select
substr(username,1,20) "user",
name "Proc Name",
count(distinct se.sid) "sessions",
sum(TOTAL_WAITS) "tot Waits",
sum(TOTAL_TIMEOUTS) "tot Timeout",
sum(TIME_WAITED) "tot Time cs",
round(avg(AVERAGE_WAIT)) "avg Time cs",
max(MAX_WAIT) "max Time cs",
event
from  v$session_event se, v$session s, v$bgprocess bp
where se.sid = s.sid(+)
and   s.paddr = bp.paddr(+)
and   event NOT like '%ipc%'
and   event NOT like 'SQL%'
and   event NOT like '%timer%'
group by username, name, event
order by username, max(MAX_WAIT) DESC
```

# Question 40:  System database in oracle

What is the System Database in Oracle?

**A.** There is no system database in oracle, just 'a database'. There is a system tablespace that every oracle database has that stores dictionary objects and is owned by sys.

# Question 41:  Unable to lock table trades

I am using oracle 8i version and I tried to execute Catldr;

When direct = false the data are uploaded

but when direct = true the following error appeared:

"SQL*Loader-908: Unable to lock table TRADES due to ORACLE error 54"

What should be done to lock table trades?

**A.** The table is busy and cannot be locked. You have to kill other sessions using the table.

## Question 42:  Exporting questionable statistics

When exporting some thing using exp (record level, table level, schema level), I am getting a warning "EXP-00091: Exporting questionable statistics". This is not the case when I export only some partitions of the table. I am using the same system as the db server is running.

What causes this warning while exporting?

**A.** Correct your nls settings or use statistics=none on the export. Or ignore the error as it isn't really important.

# Question 43: EM 10g setup

I want to setup my EM10g in the following environment:

I have three RAC databases with 2 nodes (Sun Solaris) each, one for intranet, one for internet and one for staging.

There are 6 Application Servers (Windows 2003) pointing to each node, where I plan to install iAS 10g.

Where would be the best place to install my EM to monitor 6 database instances and 6 iAS servers? Shall I install OMS on one node only and install Agents on all the nodes and iAS servers or install one OMS on each node and each iAS server?

Do I need to install Oracle Database 10g Grid Control or just Database Control?

**A.** I recommend that you install grid control on a separate server and the agent on all the others.

# Question 44:  Binary Compatibility

I need to understand something a third party application vendor
is telling me

We have a third party application currently running on Oracle
Version 9.2.0.4. The vendor wants us to upgrade to either 9.2.05
or 9.2.0.7 because one of the components this application uses is
certified on those versions. I specifically asked him as to what
was the problem they were hitting if and when they tried
certifying on Oracle Version 9.2.0.4. His respond is:

"There aren't any specific features in 9205 that are required for
router 157. The reason we require Oracle version
9205/9206/9207 is due to Oracle's statement of binary
compatibility.
We compiled Router 157 with Oracle 9205. Oracle states that our
compiled code is now compatible only with versions of Oracle
that have the same first 3 digits of the release version, and the
same or higher number in the 4th digit. 9204 has a lower
number in the 4th digit of the release, so Oracle has no statement
of binary compatibility. Simply stated... you are trying to run a
compiled version of Router with a version of Oracle older than
what we built with."

I have always tried to let the vendors control the first two digits
of Oracle Versioning for their products. The 4th digit onwards I
have always felt is Operating System specific.

We have over 85 Oracle environments and keep most of our
databases at the same release. This way it helps us keep a
standardized environment  at a manageable level.

Are there documents that would tell me about the binary
compatibility within the Oracle releases?


**A.** The vendor should always control whatversion; the 4th
number is not as specific. It fixes a number of bugs / security
issues.

If they haven't tested their app against 9.2.0.4 and you are using it, then expect problems. You should always use the version that the app has been compiled against in case the libraries have changed.

## Question 45: DB links clean up after refresh

After a database refresh, we are changing the db links in the procedures to point to the corresponding dev databases.

Is there any easy way to eliminate this tedious process?

**A.** You don't need to change anything, have tns entries for the original databases on the dev servers which point to the dev databases. Also, a synonym on db_link works well.

## Question 46: Oracle failsafe over distances

There are 2 nodes separated over 1 mile. It's an active/passive scenario.

Can you use Oracle failsafe across distances? If so, does this degrade performance?

**A.** As the Oracle Fail Safe is based on the Microsoft Windows Cluster, the nodes need to have shared storage so both nodes can access the disks. So the performance depends on what kind of network you would use to connect the hosts and the disks. If you need a disaster recovery solution better go with a standby database on the remote location o. This would not make any performance problem on the primary DB.

I suggest you go to the oracle clinic for quick and easy Oracle database support and consulting.

## Question 47: Accessing 2 databases (10g) on Win XP

I have created two databases with Oracle 10g on a single PC. The first was done at install and the second with database assistant.

Enterprise manager (also called Database Control) is always accessing the first database even ORACLE_SID is set to the second database in registry.

Do I have to type another address than http://localhost:1158/em to access the second database?

**A.** Check %ORACLE_HOME%\install\portlist.ini.
That file will tell you which port number is using for which instance.

Otherwise, you can find in the browser the following address filled in the address bar:

http://localhost:1158/em/console/database/instance/sitemap?event=doLoad&target=base1&type=oracle_database;

Create a copy of the link for OEM, put this url in the "URL" field on the link, changed "base1" to "base2". You will get a correct link to open OEM for "base2".

Starting and shutting down the correct database (or both) may be done with SQL*Plus, connect sys/psw@base1 (or 2) as sysdba, then startup or shutdown.

# Question 48:  Partitions of table

I want to know if I can place partitions of a single table into multiple tablespaces?  If so, what is the correct syntax for doing this?

**A.** Yes, you can place partitions of a single table into multiple tablespaces.

Here is an example of range partitioned table:

```
CREATE TABLE invoices
(invoice_no NUMBER NOT NULL,
invoice_date DATE NOT NULL,
comments VARCHAR2(500))
PARTITION BY RANGE (invoice_date)
(PARTITION invoices_q1 VALUES LESS THAN
(TO_DATE('01/04/2001', 'DD/MM/YYYY')) TABLESPACE
users1,
PARTITION invoices_q2 VALUES LESS THAN
(TO_DATE('01/07/2001', 'DD/MM/YYYY')) TABLESPACE
users2,
PARTITION invoices_q3 VALUES LESS THAN
(TO_DATE('01/09/2001', 'DD/MM/YYYY')) TABLESPACE
users3,
PARTITION invoices_q4 VALUES LESS THAN
(TO_DATE('01/01/2002', 'DD/MM/YYYY')) TABLESPACE
users4);
```

Hash partitioning:

```
CREATE TABLE invoices
(invoice_no NUMBER NOT NULL,
invoice_date DATE NOT NULL,
comments VARCHAR2(500))
PARTITION BY HASH (invoice_no)
PARTITIONS 4
STORE IN (users1, users2, users3, users4);
```

or:

```
CREATE TABLE invoices
(invoice_no NUMBER NOT NULL,
invoice_date DATE NOT NULL,
comments VARCHAR2(500))
PARTITION BY HASH (invoice_no)
(PARTITION invoices_q1 TABLESPACE users1,
PARTITION invoices_q2 TABLESPACE users2,
PARTITION invoices_q3 TABLESPACE users3,
PARTITION invoices_q4 TABLESPACE users4);
```

You can view the complete syntax at:
http://download-uk.oracle.com/docs/...02.htm#i2095331

# Question 49: Closing the database

I am linked to a database as SYS but was not permitted to close that database. The following message showed:

SQL> alter database close;
alter database close
*
ERROR at line 1:
ORA-01093: ALTER DATABASE CLOSE only permitted with no sessions connected

How do I close the database?


**A.** You are not permitted to close database if there is at least one more session, other than the current one, logged in to the instance. ALTER DATABASE CLOSE is not permitted when other sessions are active.

Find the other sessions and disconnect them. Then reissue the ALTER DATABASE CLOSE statement. Also, issue the SHUTDOWN IMMEDIATE command to force users off the system or issue the SHUTDOWN ABORT command to shut down the database without waiting for users to be forced off.

To check if sessions are not connected:
select sid,serial#,username from v$session where username is not null

# Question 50: Change rowid

I want to do a rowid change under the following conditions:

- The row is stored in a normal heap table (not IOT, not partitioned, not clustered, not compressed)
- There is no index
- The table is locked in ROW SHARE mode
- DB version is Oracle 10gR2

I want to delete all rows which have been committed before my transaction has begun from this table. To achieve this I do the following:

1) I lock the table in ROW SHARE mode
2) I define a timestamp t1
2) I execute my transaction
3) I delete the rows which were committed at the point in time t1 with the following statement: "delete from my_table where rowid in (select rowid from my_table as of timestamp t1)"

Is there an easier way to change rowid?

**A.** The rowid will not change unless the row movement clause is enabled for that table. Do the ff:

1. Delete the whole table (this will delete just the committed rows) and it will start your transaction.
2. Do the rest your transaction.

## Question 51:   Access environment variable in an SQL Script

I have Stored Procedure on my UNIX box and need to access the environment variable defined on the UNIX box in the Stored Procedure. I am calling this stored procedure using an SQL file.

For example:

We have an environment variable called "$e2DefaultEnv" that has the value as 'TECH' and have a Stored Procedure called "createfilters" in my Oracle DB under a schema called "E2". I want to call the stored procedure as: E2.createfilters ('${e2DefaultEnv}'); exit;

Can I pass the environment name to my Stored Procedure using an SQL file?

**A.** No you can't, but you can probably use something from your UNIX box.

Make a shell script to generate the SQL code for calling the procedure then execute that SQL code in sqlplus:

make_sql.sh:

```
#!/bin/bash
echo "
spool proc.log
connect user/password@db
begin
proc($e2DefaultEnv);
end;
/
spool off
exit
" > test.sql
sqplus /nolog @test.sql
```

Then run the make_sql.sh which will create the SQL script and run it using SQL*Plus. The stored procedure in it is called proc in the example. You will have a log of the operation in the proc.log file.

## Question 52: Call stored procedure over dblink

How can we call a stored procedure over a dblink?

**A.** Use the following code:

declare

  procedure_name@dblink;

end;

/

# Question 53: Fragmentation on LMT

I'm running a 9.2.0.6. I read that LMT tablespaces should not have fragmentation since it is system managed. When I ran a query to check for tbsp fragmentation, the following results showed:

Query:

```
SELECT dfsc.tablespace_name tablespace_name,
DECODE (
dfsc.percent_extents_coalesced,
100,
(DECODE (
GREATEST ((SELECT COUNT (1)
FROM dba_free_space dfs
WHERE dfs.tablespace_name = dfsc.tablespace_name), 1),
1,
'No Frag',
'Bubble Frag'
)
),
'Possible Honey Comb Frag'
)
fragmentation_status

FROM dba_free_space_coalesced dfsc
ORDER BY dfsc.tablespace_name;
```

```
Tablespace Name Fragmentation Status
-------------------- -------------------------
CPD bubble frag
IDX no frag
AUDIT no frag
STAT bubble frag
SYSTEM bubble frag
UNDO bubble frag
```

What does "bubble frag" mean?

**A.** A "bubble frag" means you have lots of small holes around the table space. This doesn't matter as all those holes are all perfectly useable.

Fragmented means you have lots of little holes which cannot be used therefore wasting space (hence fragmented). Having lots of little holes in a tablespace isn't a problem in Oracle as long as they can be used.

# Question 54: Clone database to another machine

I have a 9.2 on NT 2003 server and need to move my existing database. The database should be exactly copied or cloned to another machine with no Oracle installed yet.

What is the right link or procedure to clone my existing database and have it transferred to another machine?

**A.** Do a backup/restore, backup from one system and restore to the other machine.

If you're in archivelog mode, you can do it hot, but then you'll have to pick a point in time at which the databases will begin to diverge. If you're in noarchivelog mode, it's even easier, just shutdown and copy everything over.

If you have MetaLink access, Doc ID 224274.1 use it to explain how to convert it to hot.

# Question 55: Insert procedure

The following code was performed:

```
CREATE TYPE TEST AS OBJECT(
TEST_ID INTEGER,
NAVN VARCHAR2)
NOT INSTANTIABLE
NOT FINAL;

CREATE TYPE DOKTEST UNDER TEST(
DOK CLOB)
FINAL;

CREATE TABLE TEST_TBL OF TEST(
PRIMARY KEY(TEST_ID));

CREATE OR REPLACE PROCEDURE SUBTEST(
SNAME VARCHAR2,
FILNAVN VARCHAR2)

IS
INNHOLD CLOB;
FIL BFILE;
BEGIN

INSERT INTO UTFLUKT_TBL VALUES(
KLATRETUR_TP(
SEQ_UTFLUKT.NEXTVAL,
SNAME,
EMPTY_CLOB()))

RETURNING DOK INTO INNHOLD;

FIL := BFILENAME('DOKUMENTER',FILNAVN);

DBMS_LOB.FILEOPEN(FIL);
DBMS_LOB.LOADFROMFILE(INNHOLD,FIL,DBMS_LOB.GE
TLENGTH(FIL));
DBMS_LOB.FILECLOSE(FIL);
```

COMMIT;
END;


RETURNING DOK INTO INNHOLD will not work because DOK exists in the subtype DOKTEST.

I also tried:
RETURNING (TREAT(VALUE(T) AS DOKTEST).DOK FROM TEST_TBL T) INTO INNHOLD;

How do I create an insert procedure with subtype clob?


**A.** Treat should work fine, but you have to alias your table when using TREAT.

Change your insert to this:

INSERT INTO UTFLUKT_TBL T VALUES(
KLATRETUR_TP(
SEQ_UTFLUKT.NEXTVAL,
SNAME,
EMPTY_CLOB()))
RETURNING TREAT(VALUE(T) AS KLATRETUR_TP).DOK
INTO INNHOLD;

## Question 56: Append values to an existing row in a nested table

I have some keywords describing a picture in a nested table.

Code example:

```
CREATE TYPE keyword_tp as OBJECT (
keyword varchar2(30));

CREATE TYPE nt_keyword_tp as table of keyword_tp;

CREATE TYPE PICTURE_TP AS OBJECT (
pictureid number(4),
title varchar2(30),
keyword nt_keyword_tp);


CREATE TABLE picture_tbl of picture_tp(
PRIMARY KEY(pictureid))
NESTED TABLE KEYWORD STORE AS keyword_nested((
(Primary key(nested_table_id, keyword))
organization index compress);


insert into bilde_tbl values(1,'fine
picture',nt_keyword_tp(keyword_tp('exampledata')));
```

How can I add / append more keywords to this row without losing the keywords that are already there?

**A.** Use the TABLE function.

Code:

```
SQL> insert into picture_tbl values (1, 'Good',
nt_keyword_tp(keyword_tp('Hello')));
```

1 row created.

SQL> commit;

Commit complete.

SQL> select * from picture_tbl;

PICTUREID TITLE
---------- -------------------------------
KEYWORD(KEYWORD)
----------------------------------------------------------------------------
---
       1 Good
NT_KEYWORD_TP(KEYWORD_TP('Hello'))

SQL> insert into table(select keyword from picture_tbl where pictureid = 1) values ('Hi');

1 row created.

SQL> commit;

Commit complete.

SQL> select * from picture_tbl;

PICTUREID TITLE
---------- -------------------------------
KEYWORD(KEYWORD)
----------------------------------------------------------------------------
---
       1 Good
NT_KEYWORD_TP(KEYWORD_TP('Hello'),
KEYWORD_TP('Hi!'))

## Question 57:   Index a document in a subtype

The following is my ddl:

```
CREATE OR REPLACE TYPE medlem_tp AS OBJECT (
personnummer NUMBER(5),
gateadresse VARCHAR2(50),
postnummer NUMBER(4),
poststed VARCHAR2(30),
anmerkning VARCHAR2(100),
navn navn_tp,
telefon telefon_tp,
epost epost_tp)
NOT INSTANTIABLE
NOT FINAL;
/
```

```
CREATE TABLE medlem OF medlem_tp (
PRIMARY KEY (personnummer))
NESTED TABLE telefon STORE AS telefon_nested((PRIMARY
KEY(NESTED_TABLE_ID, type_tlf,nummer))
ORGANIZATION INDEX COMPRESS)
NESTED TABLE epost STORE AS epost_nested((PRIMARY
KEY(NESTED_TABLE_ID, type_e,epost))
ORGANIZATION INDEX COMPRESS);
```

This is my subtype that I wish to create indexes on:

```
CREATE OR REPLACE TYPE styre_tp UNDER medlem_tp (
id_s NUMBER,
bilde BLOB,
text CLOB,
status VARCHAR2(30))
FINAL;
/
```

How do I index a document in a subtype?

**A.** Try:
create index medlem_sub_text_idx on medlem t(treat(value(t))
as styre_tp).text);

If you are making this an Oracle Text index (for keyword
searching), you will have to add the appropriate parameters after
the statement I just gave you to make it useable with the
CONTAINS function.

# Question 58: Rollback package installation

As part of the installation procedure, we are asked to create a back out script for any installations in our database.

If my installation includes package compilation, view creation, etc., I should create a script to backout the package compilation (or to compile the old package) and drop the view.

The same applies for all the changes that include operations on all DB objects (Tables, Views, Synonyms, Indexes, Partitions, DB links etc.).

Is there any standard or easier way to backout the installation?

**A.** You can create an ON DDL trigger to keep track of every DDL that's been done, and come up with a "back out" command if need be.

Oracle 10g contains the new Flashback Database functionality, which allows you to keep flashback logs and "rewind" your entire database at any time.

## Question 59: Add or change key on the registry on Oracle forms

What command/s do I use if I want to add or change some keys on the registry for reference on my database?

**A.** Apply the following steps:

1) Use the following built in package: TOOL_ENV

2) Attach D2KWUTIL.PLL to your form and then use

WIN_API_ENVIRONMENT package.

## Question 60: Dates converting to numbers

The following codes were used for my query:

select

to_number((to_date ('00:04:30','HH24:MI:SS')) -
(to_date('00:04:00','HH24:MI:SS')))

from dual;

It executed fine but I was expecting a result of 30 instead of 0.00347422.

How do I convert the elapse time into a number?

**A.** The result of DATE - DATE in Oracle is always in Days.

So you will have to modify the result number a bit:

(DATE - DATE)*24*60 --> Result converted into minutes;

# Question 61: Display first and last name

I have a list box which needs to show the first name and the last name of all customers in it; however it only displays the first name.

This is mycode in the record group:

SELECT Fname, Lname, to_char(customer_id)

FROM all_cust

ORDER BY Lname


How can I display the first and last name together?


**A.** I would suggest concatenating the first and last names as in:
SELECT Lname||', '||fname, to_char(customer_id)
FROM all_cust
ORDER BY Lname

The concatenated first and last names will be displayed and hte customer ID will be used in the database.

# Question 62: Replicate table structure

I use DDL statement to change the table's structure at master site.

How do I replicate this table at MV?

**A.** Read about dbms_metadata at:

http://www.psoug.org/reference/dbms_metadata.html;

Here is a sample code:

```
SQL> SET LONG 10000
SQL> SELECT dbms_metadata.get_ddl('TABLE', 'MY_TEMP1')
||';' AS txt
  2  FROM dual;

TXT
-------------------------------------------------------------------------------
---

  CREATE TABLE "SYSTEM"."MY_TEMP1"
   (   "OWNERA" VARCHAR2(30),
       "OWNERB" VARCHAR2(30),
       "OBJECT_NAME" VARCHAR2(128),
       "OBJECT_TYPE" VARCHAR2(18)
   ) PCTFREE 10 PCTUSED 40 INITRANS 1 MAXTRANS 255
NOCOMPRESS LOGGING
   STORAGE(INITIAL 65536 NEXT 1048576 MINEXTENTS 1
MAXEXTENTS 2147483645
   PCTINCREASE 0 FREELISTS 1 FREELIST GROUPS 1
BUFFER_POOL DEFAULT)
   TABLESPACE "USERS"
;

TXT
-------------------------------------------------------------------------------
---


SQL>
```

## Question 63: Compare contents of two tables

What command/s can be used to compare the contents of two tables?

**A.** If the tables have the same columns, use this:
select *
from table1
minus
select *
from table2;

select *
from table2
minu
select *
from table1;

It they have the same records, both queries will return no rows.

## Question 64: Copy table contents to another table

How can I properly copy contents of a table and have it transferred to another table?

**A.** If the table already exists and you simply want to copy, you can do:

insert into table_name select * from original_table_name;

If the table doesn't exist yet you can do:

create table table_name as select * from original_table_name;

If the table exists and you don't mind it being locked, and you know the foreign keys and such will validate, you can speed it up with:

insert /*+ APPEND */ into table_name select * from original_table_name;

# Question 65: Insufficient select privilege

I'm trying to create a view on v$ tables. When I do "select * from v$mystat", all records are shown from this table.

But if I do "create or replace view test_view as select * from v$mystat" I get an error "ORA-01031: insufficient privileges".

The command "create or replace view test_view as select* from v$session" works perfectly.

Are there any other privileges required to create a view in my schema?

**A.** Try this code:

connect "/ as sysdba"

grant select on V_$mystat to johndoe;

connect johndoe/johndoe@yourdb

create or replace view test_view as select * from v$mystat;


Note that V$MYSTAT is a synonym that points to

SYS.V_$MYSTAT.

You need to grant select on V_$MYSTAT.

# Question 66: TNS

Assume this query to connect to the database:

"system/manager@MYDB"

Is there any view where I can find "MYDB"?

**A.** What you call TNS or "@mydba" is called a connect string. When you use this string external to Oracle it identifies an Oracle instance. Each Oracle instance has a name and the Connect string contains values that describe the desired Oracle instance to the network so that a connection can be made. The connect string parameter values are contained in a file called Tnsnames.ora, generally located in the /oracle_home/network/admin directory. The connect string is also used to connect to a different instance in Oracle.

The "@mydba" string is also used when writing an SQL statement. In this case it is use to tell Oracle which instance contains the desired data source. The string used in an SQL statement is called a Database Link. This is a designation set up in Oracle's data dictionary. You can identify the database link parameters by querying a data dictionary table called Dba_db_links.

# Question 67: Executing script for Enterprise Manager

We are installing 10g on XP Pro. The original install failed but I was able to delete and re-create the default database, and then logon onto SQL*Plus. However, I was not able to bring up Enterprise Mgr in my web browser using the web address http://localhost:5500/em.

During the original install of Oracle, I received the following error:

Exterprise Manager Configuration failed
job_queue_processes must be >= 1
fix errors
Run Enterprise Manager Assistant in stand-alone mode.
You can retry configuring this database with Enterprise Manager later by manually running
c:\oracle\product\10.1.0\db_1\bin\emca.

I'm not sure what it means by stand alone mode, but I went into the c:\oracle\product\10.1.0\db_1\bin directory and logged onto SQL*Plus from there, and tried running the emca.bat script, but received the following errors:

SP2-0310: unable to open file "echo.sql"
SP2-0735: unknown SET option beginning "OH=C:\orac..."
SP2-0735: unknown SET option beginning "JRE_JAVA=%..."
SP2-0735: unknown SET option beginning "EMCA_JAR=%..."
SP2-0735: unknown SET option beginning "LIB_DIR=%O..."
SP2-0158: unknown SET option "CLASSPATH="
SP2-0735: unknown SET option beginning "CLASSPATH=..."
SP2-0735: unknown SET option beginning "CLASSPATH=..."
SP2-0735: unknown SET option beginning "CLASSPATH=..."
SP2-0735: unknown SET option beginning "CLASSPATH=..."
SP2-0735: unknown SET option beginning "CLASSPATH=..."
SP2-0735: unknown SET option beginning "CLASSPATH=..."
SP2-0735: unknown SET option beginning "CLASSPATH=..."
SP2-0735: unknown SET option beginning "CLASSPATH=..."
SP2-0735: unknown SET option beginning "CLASSPATH=..."

SP2-0735: unknown SET option beginning "CLASSPATH=..."
SP2-0735: unknown SET option beginning "CLASSPATH=..."
SP2-0735: unknown SET option beginning "CLASSPATH=..."
SP2-0735: unknown SET option beginning "CLASSPATH=..."
SP2-0735: unknown SET option beginning "CLASSPATH=..."
SP2-0734: unknown command beginning "%JRE_JAVA%..." -
rest of line ignored.

This is the emca.bat script:

```
@echo off
set OH=C:\oracle\product\10.1.0\Db_1
set JRE_JAVA=%OH%\jdk\jre\bin\java
set EMCA_JAR=%OH%\jlib\emca.jar
set LIB_DIR=%OH%\jlib
set CLASSPATH=
set CLASSPATH=%CLASSPATH%;%EMCA_JAR%;
set CLASSPATH=%CLASSPATH%%LIB_DIR%\srvm.jar;
set CLASSPATH=%CLASSPATH%%LIB_DIR%\srvmasm.jar;
set
CLASSPATH=%CLASSPATH%%LIB_DIR%\emConfigInstall.jar
;
set CLASSPATH=%CLASSPATH%%LIB_DIR%\ldapjclnt10.jar;
set CLASSPATH=%CLASSPATH%%LIB_DIR%\ldap.jar;
set CLASSPATH=%CLASSPATH%%LIB_DIR%\share.jar;
set CLASSPATH=%CLASSPATH%%LIB_DIR%\srvmhas.jar;
set
CLASSPATH=%CLASSPATH%%LIB_DIR%\oraclepki103.jar;
set CLASSPATH=%CLASSPATH%%OH%\lib\xmlparserv2.jar;
set
CLASSPATH=%CLASSPATH%%OH%\oc4j\j2ee\home\oc4j.jar;
set
CLASSPATH=%CLASSPATH%%OH%\assistants\jlib\assistants
Common.jar;
set
CLASSPATH=%CLASSPATH%%OH%\sysman\jlib\emCORE.jar
;
set
CLASSPATH=%CLASSPATH%%OH%\oui\jlib\OraInstaller.jar;
%JRE_JAVA% -classpath %CLASSPATH% -
DDISPLAY=%DISPLAY% -DORACLE_HOME=%OH% -
DTNS_ADMIN=%TNS_ADMIN%
oracle.sysman.emcp.EMConfigAssistant %*
```

What is the correct procedure to run Enterprise Manager?

**A.** Run your emca.bat script on windows and not on sqlplus.

To run Enterprise Manager Configuration Assistant in stand alone mode,
Execute: Start>All Programs> {Your Oracle Home}>Configuration and Migration Tools>Enterprise Manager Configuration Assistant

# Question 68:   Updating partition key column

When I updated the table based on the leading partition key, I got the following error message:

ORA-14402: updating partition key column would cause a partition change

Then, I changed the table to:

alter table inventory ENABLE ROW MOVEMENT;

Now it works fine. I have two questions though:

1. When we update the partition key, does Oracle really move the data to different partition or it deletes the record in current partition and insert into another partition?

2. Do we incur extra cost when we update partition key?


**A.** 1. They are the same as move = delete + insert.

2. Yes, you're not just updating a single column and leaving the row in place, you're actually moving the row to a new block. You're also requiring that two partitions of every local index be modified.

## Question 69: Shared pool memory

How many memory layers are found in the shared pool?

**A.** The shared pool portion of the SGA contains three major areas: library cache, dictionary cache, buffers for parallel execution messages, and control structures.

Shared pool consists of 2 memory layers-library cache and data dictionary cache. The library cache -contains parsed sql statements, cursor information, execution plans data dictionary cache -user account information, privileges information, data file, segment and extent information stored into the data dictionary cache.

## Question 70: Materialized views

What are materialized views? When are they used?

**A.** Materialized view is like a view but stores both definitions of a view plus the rows resulting from execution of the view. It uses a query as the bases and the query are executed at the time the view is created and the results are stored in a table. You can define the Materialized view with the same storage parameter as any other table and place it in any tablespace of your choice. You can also index and partition the Materialized view table like other tables to improve performance of queries executed against them.

Use of Materialized view:

Expensive operations such as joins and aggregations need not be executed again. If the query is satisfied with data in a Materialized view, the server transforms the query to reference the view rather than the base tables.

# Question 71: Functional index

What is a functional index?


**A.** Function-based indexes can use any Function or Object method that is declared as repeatable.

Queries using expressions can use the index.
Ex: - CREATE INDEX sales_margin_inx
ON sales (revenue - cost);


Sql> SELECT ordid
FROM sales
WHERE (revenue - cost) > 1000;


We have to enable Function-based indexes by enabling the following initialization parameters:

ALTER SESSION SET QUERY_REWRITE_ENABLED = TRUE;

ALTER SESSION SET QUERY_REWRITE_INTEGRITY = TRUSTED;

## Question 72: Components of physical database structure

What are the components of a physical database structure of Oracle database?

**A.** The physical components of oracle database are control files; redo log files and data files.

Control file: control file is read in the mount state of database. It is a small binary file which records the physical structure of database which includes:
- database name
- names and locations of data files and online redo log files.
- timestamp of database creation
- check point information
- current log sequence number.

Redo log files: This file saves all the changes that are made to the database as they occur. This plays a great role in the database recovery.

Data files: data files are the physical files which stores data of all logical structure.

## Question 73: Components of logical database structure

What are the components of a logical database structure of Oracle database?

**A.** The components are table space, segments, extents and data blocks.

A logical unit of storage of a database is called table space.

Segments are a space allocated for a specific logical storage structure within a table space.

Extents: Space allocated to a segments.

Data blocks: Oracle server manages the storage space in the data files in units is called data blocks or oracle blocks.

## Question 74: Database size

How can we determine the size of the database?

**A.** Use the following code:

select (select sum(bytes/1024/1024/1024) from v$datafile) +( select sum(bytes/1024/1024/1024) from v$tempfile) + (select sum(bytes/1024/1024/1024) from v$log) "Size of Database in GB" from dual

# Question 75: Oracle index

What is an Oracle index?

**A.** An Index is a tree structure that allows direct access to a row in a table. Indexes can be classified based on their logical design or on their physical implementation.

The logical classification groups indexes from an application perspective, while the physical classification is derived from the way the indexes are stored

Index is a schema object that can speed up the retrieval of rows by using pointers. If you do not have an index, then a full table scan occurs. Its purpose is to reduce disk I/O by using an indexed path to locate data quickly. If a table is dropped, the corresponding indexes are also dropped.

# Question 76: Private synonym

What is a private synonym?

**A.** A private synonym is owned by a specific user who has control over its availability to others.

To create a private synonym in your own schema, you must have CREATE SYNONYM system privilege.

To create a private synonym in another user's schema, you must have CREATE ANY SYNONYM system privilege.

To create a PUBLIC synonym, you must have CREATE PUBLIC SYNONYM system privilege.

Use the CREATE SYNONYM statement to create a synonym, which is an alternative name for a table, view, sequence, procedure, stored function, package, materialized view, Java class schema object, user-defined object type, or another synonym.

Synonyms provide both data independence and location transparency. Synonyms permit applications to function without modification regardless of which user owns the table or view and regardless of which database holds the table or view. However, synonyms are not a substitute for privileges on database objects. Such privileges must be granted to a user before the user can use the synonym.

# Question 77:  View

What is an Oracle view?

**A.** A view is a named query. It is a tailored presentation of the data contained in one or more tables (or other views).

For SQL, view = a named or derived virtual table
• For users, view = a table (which in fact does not exist!)
• View [1] = a separate copy of an underlying table
• View = a window into the underlying table
• Changes can be done from both directions:
underlying table « view

Views are created, dropped or granted access to, identical to a table.

# Question 78: Schema objects

What are Schema Objects?

**A.** A schema is a collection of database objects. It is owned by a database user and has the same name as that user. Schema objects are logical structures created by users. Objects may define areas of the database to hold data, such as tables or indexes, or may consist just of a definition, such as a views or synonyms.

There is no relationship between a tablespace and a schema. Objects in the same schema can use storage in different tablespaces, and a tablespace can contain data from different schemas.

Schema objects can be created and manipulated using SQL. As an administrator, you can create and manipulate schema objects, just as you do with the logical and physical structures of your database using Oracle Enterprise Manager. The underlying SQL is generated for you by Oracle Enterprise Manager.

# Question 79: System tablespace

What is system tablespace and when is it created?

**A.** System tablespace is the memory allocated by oracle for creation of objects, views and indexes.

This is created automatically by oracle when the Database is created.

SYSTEM TABLESPACE USAGE NOTES:
Username - Name of the user
Created - User creation date
Profile - Name of resource profile assigned to the user
Default Tablespace - Default tablespace for data objects
Temporary Tablespace - Default tablespace for temporary objects

Only SYS, SYSTEM and possibly DBSNMP should have their default tablespace set to SYSTEM.

select USERNAME,
CREATED,
PROFILE,
DEFAULT_TABLESPACE,
TEMPORARY_TABLESPACE
from dba_users
order by USERNAME

Objects in SYSTEM TS
OBJECTS IN SYSTEM TABLESPACE NOTES:

Owner - Owner of the object
Object Name - Name of object
Object Type - Type of object
Tablespace - Tablespace name
Size - Size (bytes) of object

Any user (other than SYS, SYSTEM) should have their objects moved out of the SYSTEM tablespace.

```
select OWNER,
SEGMENT_NAME,
SEGMENT_TYPE,
TABLESPACE_NAME,
BYTES
from dba_segments
where TABLESPACE_NAME = 'SYSTEM'
and OWNER not in ('SYS','SYSTEM')
order by OWNER, SEGMENT_NAME
```

# Question 80: Rename a database

How do you rename a database?

**A.** For this script to run properly do the following:

-- Backup the Control file to Trace
ALTER DATABASE BACKUP CONTROLFILE TO TRACE;

-- Shutdown the database to make the changes
SHUTDOWN IMMEDI ATE;

-- Edit the trace file and change the CREATE CONTROLFILE
command
-- CREATE CONTROLFILE REUSE SET DATABASE
"NEW_SID_NAME" RESETLOGS
-- (note the SET keyword)

Change the name in Control file and Init.ora
The first line of Control file should b e "CREATE CONTROLFILE
REUSE SET DATABASE "" RESETLOGS ARCHIVELOG"

- modify the db_name parameter in the init.ora

-- Startup the datbase nomount with changed PFile
STARTUP NOMOUNT;

-- Execute the create controlfile command.
@create_control.sql;

-- Cancel base recovery of the database
Recover database USING BACKUP CONTROLFILE until cancel;
CANCEL

-- Open resetlogs of the database
ALTER DATABASE OPEN RESETLOGS;

-- Rename GLOBAL_NAME to

ALTER DATABASE RENAME GLOBAL_NAME TO ;

-- Create SPFile, if required give NAME and PATH of the PFILE
CREATE SPFILE FROM PFILE;

Select name from v$database;

# Question 81:  New features of Oracle 9i

What are the new features of Oracle 9i?

**A.** The oracle 9i has new features such as:
1. Dynamic Memory Management
2. Default tablespace at the db level
3. Temporary tablespace at the dba level
4. Undo tablespace management (auto/manual)

## Question 82: Relationship among database, tablespace and data file

What are the relationships among database, tablespace and data file?

**A.** Databases, tablespaces and datafiles are closely related, but they have important differences:

--- An Oracle Database consists of one or more tablespaces

--- Each Table space in an Oracle database consists of one or more files
   called datafiles.

--- A database's data is collectively stored in the datafiles that constitute
   each tablespace of the database.

# Question 83: Virtual Index

What are the characteristics of a Virtual Index?

**A:** Virtual Index characteristics are as follows:

1. Virtual indexare permanent and continue to exist unless we drop them.

2. Their creation will not affect existing and new sessions. Only sessions marked for Virtual Index usage will become aware of their existence.

3. Such indexes will be used only when the hidden parameter "_use_nosegment_indexes" is set to true.

4. The Rule based optimizer did not recognize Virtual Indexes but CBO recognizes them.

5. Dictionary view DBA_SEGMENTS will not show an entry for Virtual Indexes. The table DBA_INDEXES and DBA_OBJECTS will have an entry for them in Oracle 8i; in Oracle 9i onwards, DBA_INDEXES no longer show Virtual Indexes.

6. Virtual Indexes cannot be altered and throw a "fake index" error!

7. Virtual Indexes can be analyzed, using the ANALYZE command or DBMS_STATS package, but the statistics cannot be viewed (in Oracle 8i, DBA_INDEXES will not show this either). Oracle may be generating artificial statistics and storing it somewhere for referring it later.
Creating a Virtual Index can be achieved by using the NOSEGMENT clause with the CREATE INDEX command.

# Question 84: Hash clusters

When is hash cluster useful?

**A.** Hash clusters are useful in cases when:

1. There is a uniform, even and predictable no. of key values.

2. Queries using equality predicates.

3. The table is NOT growing constantly, and the keys are rarely updated.

# Question 85: SQL* Plus

I am using sql*plus to connect to the database on the local machine.
The database is on the same host so I don't have a connect string.

What should I specify in the HOST test box if I try to login as sys?

**A.** Put the instance name in there.

# Question 86: Shared Pool Size threshold

Currently, the shared pool size is 168 MB and the hit ratio is 78%.

How do I increase the shared pool size to arrive >90% hit ratio?

**A.** Either increase shared_pool or Tune SQL. Shared pool can be increased dynamically using alter system set shared_pool_size=, but first you need to check, if there is a free space available using v$sga_dynamic_free_memory.

Check first where the problem is:
1) misses (reload/pin ratio)
2) gethit/gets ratio, pinhit/pins ratio
3) invalidations
4) large Anonymous blocks
5) shared pools reserved

# Question 87: Cumulative Backup problem

My database is fast growing with about 50GB of current size. I do a nightly cumulative backup, including the archive logs using the following script:

allocate channel oem_backup_disk1 type disk format 'd:\\mad3_nightly_backups\\%U';
backup incremental level 1 cumulative as BACKUPSET tag '%TAG' database include current controlfile;
recover copy of database;
backup as BACKUPSET tag '%TAG' archivelog all not backed up delete all input;
report obsolete;
crosscheck backup;
crosscheck copy;
report need backup;
report unrecoverable;
release channel oem_backup_disk1;

I have been running this for a week now but each night the total backup size is about 45GB. To satisfy the retention policy of 1 day, I have to keep last 6 days of backup (according to RMAN report). That is about 250GB.

Below is my RMAN configuration:

RETENTION POLICY TO REDUNDANCY 1; # default
BACKUP OPTIMIZATION OFF; # default
DEFAULT DEVICE TYPE TO DISK; # default
CONTROLFILE AUTOBACKUP OFF; # default
CONTROLFILE AUTOBACKUP FORMAT FOR DEVICE TYPE DISK TO '%F'; # default
DEVICE TYPE DISK PARALLELISM 1 BACKUP TYPE TO BACKUPSET; # default
DATAFILE BACKUP COPIES FOR DEVICE TYPE DISK TO 1; # default
ARCHIVELOG BACKUP COPIES FOR DEVICE TYPE DISK TO

1; # default
MAXSETSIZE TO UNLIMITED; # default
ENCRYPTION FOR DATABASE OFF; # default
ENCRYPTION ALGORITHM 'AES128'; # default
ARCHIVELOG DELETION POLICY TO NONE; # default
SNAPSHOT CONTROLFILE NAME TO
'C:\ORACLE\PRODUCT\10.2.0\DB_1\DATABASE\S....

What is the proper procedure to make a cumulative backup?

**A.** I see the "recover copy of database" in there. Are you trying to use the new 10g feature that puts incremental backups right into the backed up files?

To do that, you must be using COPY, not BACKUPSET. In 10g, if you do a full COPY of database at incremental level 0, you can then do incremental level 1 copies that actually merge into your level 0 instead of creating new backup files every night.

For updated backups, visit: http://www.oracle-base.com/articles/10g/RM

# Question 88: Failing scheduled Oracle-Suggested Backup

I have setup a backup job using the 'Scheduled Oracle-Suggested Backup' in 10g every night. The first run was successful but from the second night it started to fail.

I'm using ASM and the output log shows the following:

Recovery Manager: Release 10.2.0.1.0 - Production on Sun Apr 2 20:00:29 2006
Copyright © 1982, 2005, Oracle. All rights reserved.

RMAN>
connected to target database: MAD3 (DBID=2368746663)
using target database control file instead of recovery catalog
RMAN>
echo set on

RMAN> run {
2> allocate channel oem_disk_backup device type disk;
3> recover copy of database with tag 'ORA$OEM_LEVEL_0';
4> backup incremental level 1 cumulative copies=1 for recover of copy with tag 'ORA$OEM_LEVEL_0' database;
5> }
allocated channel: oem_disk_backup
channel oem_disk_backup: sid=147 devtype=DISK

Starting recover at 02-APR-06
no copy of datafile 6 found to recover
no copy of datafile 7 found to recover
no copy of datafile 8 found to recover
no copy of datafile 9 found to recover
no copy of datafile 10 found to recover
no copy of datafile 11 found to recover
no copy of datafile 12 found to recover
no copy of datafile 13 found to recover
no copy of datafile 14 found to recover
no copy of datafile 15 found to recover

no copy of datafile 16 found to recover
no copy of datafile 17 found to recover
no copy of datafile 18 found to recover
no copy of datafile 19 found to recover
no copy of datafile 20 found to recover
no copy of datafile 21 found to recover
no copyof datafile 22 found to recover
no copy of datafile 23 found to recover
no copy of datafile 24 found to recover
no copy of datafile 25 found to recover
no copy of datafile 26 found to recover
no copy of datafile 27 found to recover
no copy of datafile 28 found to recover
no copy of datafile 29 found to recover
no copy of datafile 30 found to recover
no copy of datafile 31 found to recover
channel oem_disk_backup: starting incremental datafile
backupset restore
channel oem_disk_backup: specifying datafile copies to recover
recovering datafile copy fno=00001
name=+MAD3ASM/mad3/datafile/system.392.586209619
recovering datafile copy fno=00002
name=+MAD3ASM/mad3/datafile/undotbs1.395.586209667
recovering datafile copy fno=00003
name=+MAD3ASM/mad3/datafile/sysaux391.586209645
recovering datafile copy fno=00004
name=+MAD3ASM/mad3/datafile/users.396.586209669
recovering datafile copy fno=00005
name=+MAD3ASM/mad3/datafile/madattrib.768.586383235
channel oem_disk_backup: reading from backup piece
+MAD3ASM/mad3/backupset/2006_03_31/nnndn1_tag20060
331t200142_0.2759.586555651
released channel: oem_disk_backup
RMAN-00571:
===============================================
===============
RMAN-00569: =============== ERROR MESSAGE STACK
FOLLOWS ===============
RMAN-00571:
===============================================
===============

RMAN-03002: failure of recover command at 04/02/2006
20:00:41

ORA-19870: error reading backup piece
+MAD3ASM/mad3/backupset/2006_03_31/nnndn1_tag20060
331t200142_0.2759.586555651
ORA-19809: limit exceeded for recovery files
ORA-19804: cannot reclaim 157286400 bytes disk space from
2147483648 limit

RMAN> exit;
Recovery Manager complete.

Why is the 'Scheduled Oracle-Suggested Backup' failing?

**A.** I see two possible issues here.

The first is ORA-19809 down at the bottom, which you have to
change the parameter DB_RECOVERY_FILE_DEST_SIZE to
fix.

The other is the "no copy of datafile # found to recover" This may
be related to the fact that you're not b acking up fully (because of
the 19809 error), but it is could also be:

1) Your incremental backup is going bad and you must do a full
backup incremental level 0. Even though the new method of
"recovering into the datafile copy" is a nice one, it's still not a
perfect datafile at times.

2) Have you done a "alter database open resetlogs" lately? This
can cause issues with the new datafile copy backup method.

## Question 89: Diverting new data to a second file

Our Oracle9i customer insists we create a second datafile on a different volume to overcome a space issue.

What is the effect of removing autoextend from the first datafile had and what will happen when table indexes in the first datafile expand?

**A.** When autoextend is removed from the table it will automatically store data in second datafile if extents are free in same or autoextend is on in second DF. Index will have no effect.

## Question 90: File types supported by SQL*Loader

What are the different file types that are supported by SQL*Loader?

**A:** There are two types:

1. Direct method (skips dbcache, no redo generation)

2. Conventional method (just opposite of direct load)

## Question 91:  Size of database

How can we determine the size of the database?

**A:** Use:
select (select sum (bytes/1024/1024/1024) from v$datafile) + ( select

sum(bytes/1024/1024/1024) from v$tempfile) + (select

sum(bytes/1024/1024/1024) from v$log) "Size of Database in GB" from dual.

## Question 92:  Database w/out SPFile

Can you start a database without SPfile in oracle 9i?

**A.** Yes, it is possible to start the database using init.ora file only. The main advantage of using the SPFILE.ora is only to make changes to the dynamic initialization parameters without restarting the database using the SCOPE option. The changes will be stored in the spfile only and if you start the database using "pfile" option those changes won't be applicable to the database.

## Question 93:   Bitmap index

Where do we use bitmap index?

**A.** We can use bitmap index where cardinality is very low like gender column or color column.

## Question 94:   Advantage of using DBCA

What are the advantages of using DBCA?

**A.** The Database Configuration Assistant guides you through the process of creating a new database, changing the configuration of an existing database, or deleting a database.

Many of the database creation tasks you would normally perform manually are performed automatically after you select your database options with the Database Configuration Assistant. With the Database Configuration Assistant you can select from a list of pre-defined database templates, or you can use an existing database as a sample for creating a template. If you are using Real Application Clusters, you can use the Database Configuration Assistant to manage the instances and services associated with your Real Application Cluster environment.

Note: Oracle recommends that you close other applications when running Database Configuration Assistant.

# Question 95: Physical database structure

What are the components of a physical database structure?

**A.** Oracle database physical structure contains:

1. Data files -- always occupy the declared size on the hard disk irrespective of the rows contained in them (.dbf). The data files contain:
   - Data blocks -- smallest unit of I/O. each block contains a header
   - ROWID -- two byte pseudo column to identifyphysical location of a row
   - Table clusters -- tables which are often used together in queries are physically grouped in same data block. Cluster tables are joined on 'cluster key' which identifies the common column between the two tables.
2. Online redo log files (.rdo and .arc)
3. Control files -- contain one slot per data file declared for a database.
   Also contain other configuration parameters. (.ctl)
4. Password files.
5. sidALTR.log files -- log critical failures
6. Trace files -- saves user session traces (.trc)

# Question 96: CASE expression and statement

What is the difference between case expression and case statement?

**A.** CASE Expressions and Statements:

The CASE expression was first added to SQL in Oracle8i. Oracle9i extends its support to PL/SQL to allow CASE to be used as an expression or statement:

Value Match CASE Expression

The CASE expression is a more flexible version of the DECODE function. In its simplest form it is used to return a value when a match is found:

SELECT ename, empno, (CASE deptno   WHEN 10 THEN 'Accounting'   WHEN 20 THEN 'Research'   WHEN 30 THEN 'Sales'   WHEN 40 THEN 'Operations'   ELSE 'Unknown' END) departmentFROM empORDER BY ename;The value match CASE expression is also supported in PL/SQL:

SET SERVEROUTPUT ONDECLARE deptno   NUMBER := 20; dept_desc VARCHAR2(20);BEGIN   dept_desc := CASE deptno WHEN 10 THEN 'Accounting'        WHEN 20 THEN 'Research'        WHEN 30 THEN 'Sales'        WHEN 40 THEN 'Operations'        ELSE 'Unknown'        END; DBMS_OUTPUT.PUT_LINE(dept_desc);END;/Searched CASE Expression
A more complex version is the searched CASE expression where a comparison expression is used to find a match. In this form the comparison is not limited to a single column:

SELECT ename, empno, (CASE   WHEN sal < 1000 THEN 'Low'   WHEN sal BETWEEN 1000 AND 3000 THEN 'Medium' WHEN sal > 3000 THEN 'High'   ELSE 'N/A' END)

salaryFROM empORDER BY ename;The searched CASE
expression is also supported in PL/SQL:

SET SERVEROUTPUT ONDECLARE sal    NUMBER := 2000;
sal_desc VARCHAR2(20);BEGIN   sal_desc := CASE
WHEN sal < 1000 THEN 'Low'          WHEN sal BETWEEN
1000 AND 3000 THEN 'Medium'          WHEN sal > 3000
THEN 'High'          ELSE 'N/A'          END;
DBMS_OUTPUT.PUT_LINE(sal_desc);END;/Value Match
CASE Statement
The CASE statement supported by PL/SQL is very similar to the
CASE expression. The main difference is that the statement is
finished with an END CASE statement rather than just END. The
PL/SQL statements are essentially an alternative to lists of IF...
THEN... ELSE, IF statements:

SET SERVEROUTPUT ONBEGIN  FOR cur_rec IN (SELECT
ename, empno, deptno FROM emp ORDER BY ename) LOOP
DBMS_OUTPUT.PUT(cur_rec.ename || ' : ' || cur_rec.empno ||
' : ');   CASE cur_rec.deptno    WHEN 10 THEN
DBMS_OUTPUT.PUT_LINE('Accounting');    WHEN 20 THEN
DBMS_OUTPUT.PUT_LINE('Research');    WHEN 30 THEN
DBMS_OUTPUT.PUT_LINE('Sales');    WHEN 40 THEN
DBMS_OUTPUT.PUT_LINE('Operations');    ELSE
DBMS_OUTPUT.PUT_LINE('Unknown');    END CASE;  END
LOOP;END;/Searched CASE Statement
As with its expression counterpart, the searched CASE statement
allows multiple comparisons using multiple variables:

SET SERVEROUTPUT ONBEGIN  FOR cur_rec IN (SELECT
ename, empno, sal FROM emp ORDER BY ename) LOOP
DBMS_OUTPUT.PUT(cur_rec.ename || ' : ' || cur_rec.empno ||
' : ');   CASE    WHEN cur_rec.sal < 1000 THEN
DBMS_OUTPUT.PUT_LINE('Low');    WHEN cur_rec.sal
BETWEEN 1000 AND 3000 THEN
DBMS_OUTPUT.PUT_LINE('Medium');    WHEN cur_rec.sal
> 3000 THEN      DBMS_OUTPUT.PUT_LINE('High');
ELSE      DBMS_OUTPUT.PUT_LINE('Unknown');    END
CASE;  END LOOP;END;/

# Question 97: Integrity constraint

What is an integrity constraint?

**A.** An integrity constraint is a rule that restricts the values in a database.

There are six types:
1. A NOT NULL constraint prohibits a database value from being null.

2. A unique constraint prohibits multiple rows from having the same value
   in the same column or combination of columns but allows some to be null.

3. A primary key constraint combines a NOT NULL constraint and a unique
   constraint in a single declaration. That is, it prohibits multiple rows from
   having the same value in the same column or combination of columns
   and prohibits values from being null.

4. A foreign key constraint requires values in one table to match values in
   another table.

5. A check constraint requires a value in the database to comply with a
   specified condition.

6. A REF column by definition references an object in another object type
   or in a relational table. A REF constraint lets you further describe the
   relationship between the REF column and the object it references.

# Question 98: Correlated sub-query

What is a correlated sub-query?

**A.** A correlated sub-query is a sub-query that references the value/s from the main query.

For example:

```
SELECT colA
, colB
FROM tableA
WHERE colB < ( SELECT max(colX)
FROM tableB
WHERE tableB.colY = tableA.colA)
```

Oracle executes correlated subquery for each record from of main query, hence these types of queries have greater impact on performance and must be avoided.

# Question 99:  Access row in a table

What is the fastest way of accessing a row in a table?

**A.** The fastest way is to use ROWID.

A ROWID is created by Oracle for each new row in every table; it is a pseudo column that has a value for every row in a table. The ROWID gives us the physical address of a row and is the fastest way to access any row. The ROWID contains 3 bits of information, they are:

1. The block within the database file.
2. Row # within the block.
3. Database file ID.
An example could be:
000088C9.0191.0002

The ROWID has three important uses, these are:
1. The fastest path to any row.
2. A way of speeding the COMMIT process in application code.
3. Unique identifiers of any given row.

# Question 100: Group By and Order By

What is the difference between group by and order by?

**A.** Group by is used to get the set of records that belongs to the same group.

For Example:
Select count(empno),deptno from emp group by dept

The above statement will display number of records for each department. In the same way we can all aggregate functions like sum,avg etc.

In group by, we can select only the column(s) which are mentioned in group by clause. In above example we can't select other than deptno and aggregate functions of any other columns.

Order by displays the records either in ascending or descending order. What ever the column(s) we are mentioning in the order by clause that column(s) must exists in select clause also. We can select all other columns which are not mentioned in order by clause.

For example:
Select empno, ename,deptno from emp order by ename.

ename must be in select clause

We can select other than ename also, but we can't use any aggregate functions here.

# Index